Farm Animals

Horses on the Farm

by Bizzy Harris

Bullfrog Books

Ideas for Parents and Teachers

Bullfrog Books let children practice reading informational text at the earliest reading levels. Repetition, familiar words, and photo labels support early readers.

Before Reading

- Discuss the cover photo. What does it tell them?
- Look at the picture glossary together. Read and discuss the words.

Read the Book

- "Walk" through the book and look at the photos. Let the child ask questions. Point out the photo labels.
- Read the book to the child, or have him or her read independently.

After Reading

- Prompt the child to think more. Ask: What did you know about horses before reading this book? What more would you like to learn about them?

Bullfrog Books are published by Jump!
5357 Penn Avenue South
Minneapolis, MN 55419
www.jumplibrary.com

Library of Congress Cataloging-in-Publication Data

Names: Harris, Bizzy, author.
Title: Horses on the farm / by Bizzy Harris.
Description: Minneapolis, MN: Jump!, Inc., [2021]
Series: Farm animals | Includes index.
Audience: Ages 5–8 | Audience: Grades K–1
Identifiers: LCCN 2020021741 (print)
LCCN 2020021742 (ebook)
ISBN 9781645277095 (hardcover)
ISBN 9781645277101 (ebook)
Subjects: LCSH: Horses—Juvenile literature.
Livestock—Juvenile literature.
Classification: LCC SF302 .H395 2021 (print)
LCC SF302 (ebook) | DDC 636.1—dc23
LC record available at https://lccn.loc.gov/2020021741
LC ebook record available at https://lccn.loc.gov/2020021742

Editor: Eliza Leahy
Designer: Molly Ballanger

Photo Credits: Kerrick/iStock, cover (left); Olga Salt/Shutterstock, cover (middle); Grigorita Ko/Shutterstock, cover (right); Vasyl Syniuk/Shutterstock, 1; Eric Isselee/Shutterstock, 3, 22, 24; acceptphoto/Shutterstock, 4, 5, 23tr, 23bm; Sgoodwin4813/Dreamstime, 6–7, 23br; imageBROKER/SuperStock, 8–9, 23tl; nigel baker photography/Shutterstock, 10–11; imageBROKER/Alamy, 12–13; PabloBenii/Shutterstock, 14, 15; arthorse/Shutterstock, 16–17; Marie Charouzova/Shutterstock, 17; Pipa100/Dreamstime, 18, 23tm; wakila/iStock, 19, 23bl; Julia Siomuha/Shutterstock, 20–21.

Printed in the United States of America at Corporate Graphics in North Mankato, Minnesota.

Table of Contents

Neigh and Play

The horses neigh.
They are hungry.

What do they eat?

Hay!

The farmer opens the barn.

The horses go to the pasture.

They eat grass, too.

barn
pasture

A stallion is a male horse.

This stallion is fast.

He gallops.

A mare is a female.
This foal is her baby.
Cute!

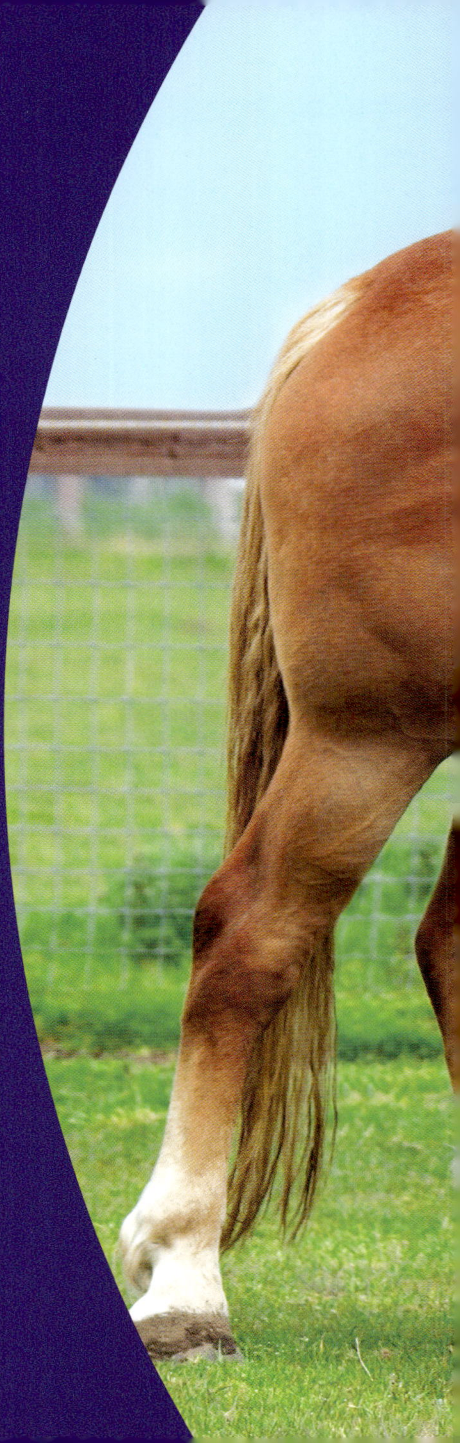

foal

Foals play.

They run and jump.

Fun!

This farmer rides a horse.

He sits in a saddle.

His feet go in stirrups.

Cool!

Horses come in many colors.

Some are spotted.

Neat!

This farmer grooms her horse.
She brushes its hair.

She cleans its hooves, too.

She cleans around each horseshoe.

The horses are tired.

Good night!

Parts of a Horse

Take a look at the parts of a horse!

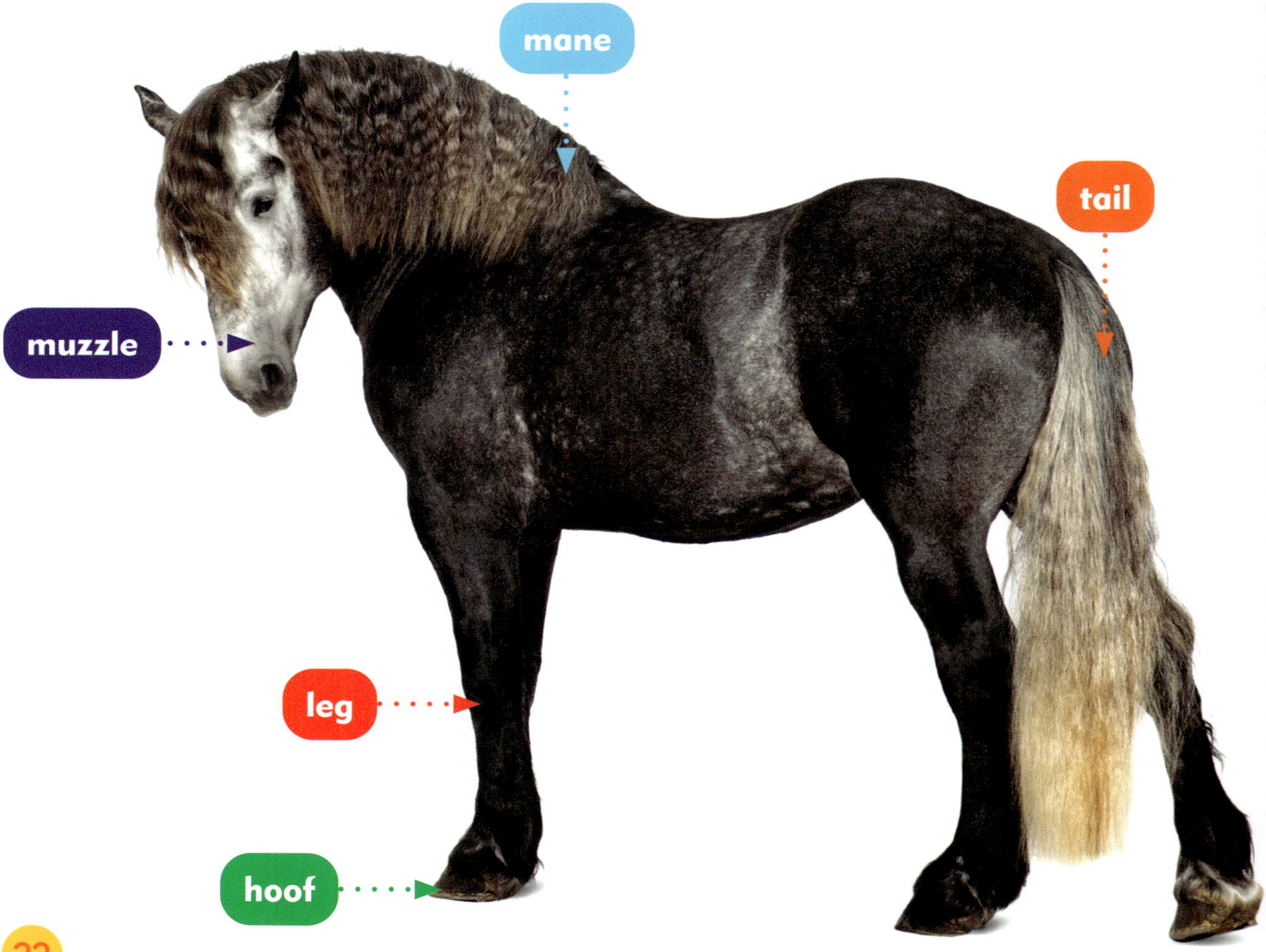

Picture Glossary

gallops
Runs fast so that all four feet are off the ground at once.

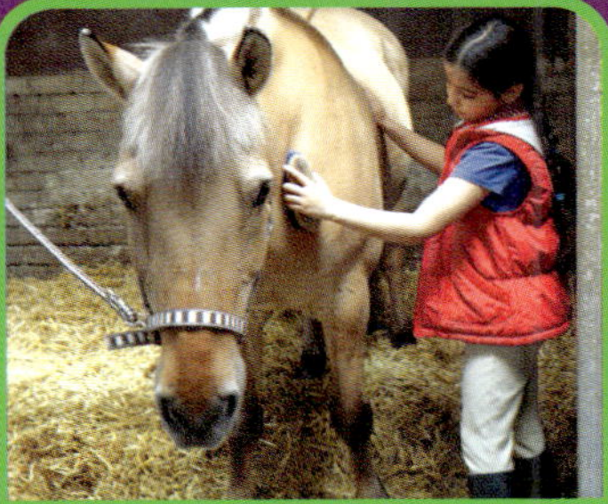

grooms
Brushes and cleans an animal.

hay
Long grass that is dried and used as food for animals.

horseshoe
A band of iron that is attached to a horse's hoof to protect it.

neigh
To make a natural noise.

pasture
Grazing land for animals.

Index

To Learn More

Finding more information is as easy as 1, 2, 3.

1. Go to www.factsurfer.com
2. Enter "horsesonthefarm" into the search box.
3. Choose your book to see a list of websites.